BEGINNER'S GUIDE TO

FAUX MOSAICS

Discover the simple, inexpensive way to create decorator mosaics! Instead of traditional ceramic tiles, our easy technique uses bits of painted illustration board. Step-by-step instructions are given for 11 STUNNING PROJECTS, but the possibilities are unlimited.

21 -22

19

15

LEISURE ARTS, INC. • Maumelle, Arkansas

BASIC INSTRUCTIONS

FOR MAKING YOUR FAUX MOSAIC PROJECT

To make your crafting of faux mosaics easier and more enjoyable, we encourage you to carefully read all of these basic instructions, study the color photographs, and familiarize yourself with the techniques before you begin.

CHOOSE YOUR MATERIALS

This section includes many of the materials and tools you need to create these intriguing projects. Most items may be found at either a hobby and craft store or an art supply store. Depending on the project you choose, it may not be necessary to have all of the supplies listed.

Base item – Many items are suitable for decorating with faux mosaics. We used items such as terra-cotta pots; a papier-mâché box; a wooden table, plate, and frame; a metal pizza pan; and a round metal tin.

Cold-press illustration board – Instead of using small ceramic tiles, you will use small pieces of painted illustration board cut into "tiles." Illustration board is available at most art supply stores and many hobby and craft stores. Make sure to ask for cold-press illustration board. This finishing process gives the board a slightly textured surface so your finished project will more closely resemble real tiles.

Thick, clear-drying craft glue – Each piece of illustration board "tile" is glued to the base item with craft glue before the spackling is applied.

Spackling – This quick-drying patching compound normally used to fill cracks and patch holes in walls is used in place of tile grout to fill in the open spaces between the illustration board "tiles." Several brands are available at local hardware and home improvement centers.

Cutting tools – A wide variety of tools may be used to cut the painted illustration board into pieces. Depending on the size and shape of the piece, you may wish to use a pair of scissors, a utility knife with a metal ruler, a paper cutter, or a rotary cutter with a cutting mat and rotary cutting ruler.

Gloss-finish clear acrylic spray sealer – Several coats of this sealer are sprayed on the painted illustration board and then on the finished project. Since it is an acrylic spray, it is very easy to use.

Acrylic paints – The illustration board is painted before it is cut into "tiles." A wide variety of acrylic paint colors is available today. Metallic colors are also readily available.

Paintbrushes – Small foam paintbrushes work well for painting your illustration board piece.

Transfer paper – Either graphite paper or Saral® transfer paper may be used to transfer your pattern.

Sandpaper – If you are using a wooden base item, you will need to sand it before painting or before gluing any illustration board pieces on the surface.

Tack cloth – This lightweight, tacky cloth is used to rub over a newly sanded wooden surface to remove all traces of sanding dust.

Stylus – Available at most art supply or craft stores, this tool is used to draw over your traced pattern when transferring a pattern to a base item. A dull pencil or a ball point pen that doesn't write also works well.

Tracing paper – You will trace the pattern onto tracing paper so that you can then transfer the pattern to your base item.

PREPARE BASE ITEM

Wood – Sand all surfaces. Remove the sanding dust with a tack cloth. If parts of the base item need to be painted because they will not be covered with a mosaic design, paint those areas now, then apply several coats of acrylic sealer to the painted areas.

Metal and Papier-mâché – For metal and papier-mâché items, no preparation is necessary if the base item is clean.

Terra-cotta pots – Apply several coats of clear acrylic spray sealer to inside of terra-cotta pots.

TRANSFER PATTERN TO BASE ITEM

Some of the designs have a pattern for a central design. If your project includes a pattern, the pattern needs to be transferred to the base item to show you where pieces are to be placed. Do not discard your pattern. It may also be used to cut specific-shaped pieces (see the rays on the Sun Face Tray or Table, pg. 19).

1. **If you are given a whole pattern**, trace pattern onto tracing paper.
   If you are given a half pattern, use a ruler to draw a line down the center of a sheet of tracing paper. Match drawn line on tracing paper to gray line on pattern. Trace pattern onto tracing paper. Turn tracing paper over, match gray line and drawn line again, and trace pattern for remaining half.

If you are given a quarter pattern, use a ruler to draw a line down the center of a sheet of tracing paper. Turn the tracing paper 90° and draw a line down the center, perpendicular to the first line. Match gray lines on pattern to drawn lines on tracing paper. Trace pattern onto tracing paper. Turn tracing paper, match gray lines and drawn lines again, and trace pattern in remaining corners.

2. Place tracing paper pattern on base item; tape in place. Place transfer paper, coated side down, between tracing paper pattern and base item. Draw over lines on tracing paper with a stylus.

PREPARE ILLUSTRATION BOARD

1. Cut illustration board to the sizes specified in the "board" column of project table. Strive for smooth, clean cuts.

2. Paint each piece of illustration board the color specified in project table. More than one coat of paint may be required for even, complete coverage.

3. Some projects require the illustration board to be sponge painted. To sponge paint, wet a piece of sea sponge; squeeze out excess water. Dip sponge in paint; do not saturate. Blot sponge on paper towel. Lightly press sponge on surface; remove sponge. Repeat to cover area.

4. When paint is completely dry, spray several light coats of the gloss-finish clear acrylic spray sealer on each piece of board.

CUT ILLUSTRATION BOARD PIECES

Illustration board pieces cut into squares, triangles, rectangles, and random-shapes are used to make up your mosaic design. The project table tells you what shapes to cut from which color. When cutting any shape (except random ones) strive for consistency when cutting. But if your measurements are slightly off, don't worry. These variations will make your finished project one of a kind. Remember, this is a free-form, expressive craft, and there are few hard and fast rules. In some cases the project table indicates a specific number of pieces to cut. Depending on how you cut your shapes and how you place them on your base item you may need more or fewer pieces. In addition, several pieces are cut into specific shapes; patterns are given for these pieces.

1. Begin by cutting painted illustration board into strips that are the size indicated in the project table as the "first cut".

2. From these strips you can cut squares, rectangles, triangles, and random-shaped pieces. Sizes and shapes are given in the project table as the "second cut". When a triangle is indicated, the measurement indicates the width of the base of the triangle and the height of the triangle at its center point (see **Fig. 1** for a ½"w x 5/8"h triangle). When random shapes are indicated, the strips may be cut into pieces any size and shape. You may also find that it is necessary to trim some pieces to fit when you place them on the base item.

Fig. 1

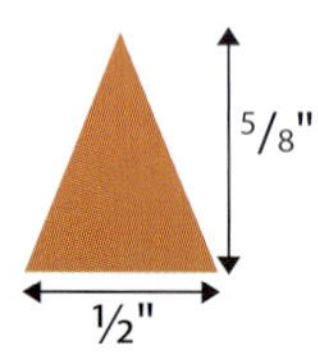

3. To cut a shape from painted illustration board using a pattern (indicated in "first cut" of project table), trace the pattern onto tracing paper. Place tracing paper pattern on illustration board. Place transfer paper, coated side down, between tracing paper pattern and illustration board. Draw over lines on tracing paper with a stylus. Carefully cut out shape.

APPLY PIECES

Now that you've prepared your base item and cut the illustration board pieces to make up the design, you are ready to apply the pieces. Again, remember that this craft is not an exact science.

As you put the pieces in place, allow approximately 1/16" between all pieces for the spackling. It will be helpful to refer to the photo (and pattern if there is one for your design) as you place your pieces on the base item.

A variety of situations may occur when applying pieces to your project. You may be placing pieces on a central design you have transferred to the base item. This may be specific-shaped pieces you have cut using the pattern (see the rays on the Sun Face Tray or Table, pg. 19) or random-shaped pieces you are using to fill an area of the transferred design (see the petals on the Daisy Flowerpot, pg. 29). Your pieces will not exactly match the transferred lines – you are simply trying to fill the general shape.

You may be placing random-shaped pieces around the central design (see the background on the Sun Face Tray or Table, pg. 19) or creating an entire area of random shapes (see the sides on the Watermelon Flowerpot, pg. 17). Applying random-shaped pieces is much like working a jigsaw puzzle. Turn the pieces and try various sides until you find the perfect pieces to lay side by side. It may be necessary to trim pieces to make them fit together.

Or, you may be placing pieces in a very specific color order to create a geometric effect (see the Geometric Frame, pg. 10).

Depending on your project, you may find it easier to glue a few pieces in place at a time or glue several. For example, when we completed a daisy design it was easier to arrange and trim a few random-shaped pieces to fit an area and glue them down before moving to the next area (see photo, right). But, for the our frame with a specific color order it was easier to lay all our pieces in place (see photo, right). At this point we assessed the fit of the pieces, moving or trimming them as necessary. When we were satisfied with the fit we removed the pieces, applied glue to the frame, and placed the pieces back on the frame. The straight edge of a small piece of illustration board was great for spreading the glue in a thin, even coat.

Depending on your placement, you may not use all the pieces cut or you may need to cut additional pieces. Pieces that are on edges should not be on the very edge of the base item; you need a bit of room for the spackling.

After determining which method works best for your project, glue all the pieces to the base item until the design is complete. Allow glue to dry overnight.

APPLY SPACKLING

1. Remove a small amount of spackling from the container. Use your fingers to apply a thin layer of spackling to the surface of your project, pushing the spackling into the areas between the pieces. Continue to apply more spackling as needed to completely fill each open area between the pieces. If you are working on a multi-sided project, you may wish to apply spackling to one side at a time.

2. When all spaces are filled, use your fingers to carefully rub and remove excess spackling from the surface of the pieces.

3. Wet a small cellulose sponge; squeeze out as much water as possible. Wipe pieces with sponge to remove any excess spackling and to remove the "haze" on the pieces.

4. Allow project to dry 2-3 hours.

5. Apply additional coats of spackling as necessary to build up the spackling to same level as illustration board pieces. Depending on the base item and your illustration board pieces, you may need as many as three coats of spackling.

APPLY SEALER

When spackling is completely dry and hardened, spray several coats of sealer on project, allowing sealer to dry between coats.

H. MATISSE

GEOMETRIC FRAME

SHOPPING LIST

- ☐ Base item – 11¼" x 11¼" wooden picture frame with 2" w flat front
- ☐ Illustration board
- ☐ Acrylic paints – black, yellow, orange, green, red, blue, and dark blue

INSTRUCTIONS

Referring to table and photo, follow Basic Instructions (pgs. 2-9) to make a faux mosaic frame.

Board	Color	First cut	Second cut
6" x 6"	Black	4 strips 3/8" x 6"	32 squares 3/8" x 3/8" and 8 rectangles 3/8" x 1"
		2 strips ½" x 6"	16 triangles 1"w x ½"h
		5 strips ¼" x 6"	44 rectangles ¼" x 5/8" for inner opening edges
		1 strip 5/8" x 6"	9 squares 5/8" x 5/8" for side edges
6" x 6"	Yellow	4 strips 3/8" x 6"	24 rectangles 3/8" x 1"
		2 strips 5/8" x 6"	10 squares 5/8" x 5/8" for side edges
6" x 6"	Orange	4 strips 3/8" x 6"	24 rectangles 3/8" x 1"
		2 strips 5/8" x 6"	9 squares 5/8" x 5/8" for side edges
5" x 6"	Green	2 strips 3/8" x 6"	8 rectangles 3/8" x 1"
		1 strip ½" x 6"	8 triangles 1"w x ½"h
		2 strips 5/8" x 6"	10 squares 5/8" x 5/8" for side edges
5" x 6"	Red	2 strips 3/8" x 6"	8 rectangles 3/8" x 1"
		1 strip ½" x 6"	8 triangles 1"w x ½"h
		2 strips 5/8" x 6"	9 squares 5/8" x 5/8" for side edges
6" x 6"	Blue	6 strips 3/8" x 6"	32 rectangles 3/8" x 1"
		2 strips 5/8" x 6"	9 squares 5/8" x 5/8" for side edges
3" x 6"	Dk Blue	2 strips 3/8" x 6"	8 rectangles 3/8" x 1"
		1 strip 5/8" x 6"	8 squares 5/8" x 5/8" for side edges

GEOMETRIC BOX

SHOPPING LIST

- ☐ Base item – 6" square papier-mâché box
- ☐ Illustration board
- ☐ Acrylic paints – black, yellow, orange, green, red, blue, and dark blue

INSTRUCTIONS

Referring to table and photo, follow Basic Instructions (pgs. 2-9) to make a faux mosaic lid. We painted the bottom of the box black.

Board	Color	First cut	Second cut
5" x 5"	Black	2 strips ½" x 5"	9 squares ½" x ½" and 8 triangles 1"w x ½"h
		2 strips 3/8" x 5"	16 squares 3/8" x 3/8"
		1 strip ¾" x 5"	7 rectangles 3/8" x ¾" for lid sides
4" x 4"	Yellow	1 strip 1" x 4"	8 rectangles 3/8" x 1"
		1 strip ¾" x 4"	7 rectangles 3/8" x ¾" for lid sides
4" x 4"	Orange	2 strips 1" x 4"	11 rectangles 3/8" x 1"
		1 strip ¾" x 4"	7 rectangles 3/8" x ¾" for lid sides
4" x 4"	Green	1 strip 1" x 4"	3 rectangles 3/8" x 1"
		1 strip ½" x 4"	4 triangles 1"w x ½"h
		1 strip ¾" x 4"	7 rectangles 3/8" x ¾" for lid sides
4" x 4"	Red	1 strip 1" x 4"	2 rectangles 3/8" x 1"
		1 strip ½" x 4"	4 triangles 1"w x ½"h
		1 strip ¾" x 4"	7 rectangles 3/8" x ¾" for lid sides
4" x 4"	Blue	2 strips 1" x 4"	12 rectangles 3/8" x 1"
		1 strip ¾" x 4"	6 rectangles 3/8" x ¾" for lid sides
4" x 4"	Dk Blue	1 strip 1" x 4"	4 rectangles 3/8" x 1"
		1 strip ¾" x 4"	7 rectangles 3/8" x ¾" for lid sides

WATERMELON TIN

SHOPPING LIST

- ☐ Base Item – 8" dia metal tin with lid
- ☐ Illustration board
- ☐ Acrylic paints – dark green, green, light green, white, pink, dark pink, and black

INSTRUCTIONS

Referring to table and photo, follow Basic Instructions (pgs. 2-9) to make a faux mosaic lid. To complete tin, we painted the sides of tin dark green and sponge painted the sides with green.

Board	Color	First cut	Second cut
3" x 8"	Dk green sponged with green	3 strips ½" x 8"	42 squares ½" x ½" for side of rim
2½" x 8"	Dk green sponged with green & lt green	3 strips 3/8" x 8"	49 squares 3/8" x 3/8" for rind
2" x 6"	Lt green	3 strips ¼" x 6"	54 squares ¼" x ¼" for rind
2" x 6"	White	3 strips ¼" x 6"	49 squares ¼" x ¼" for rind
4" x 6"	Pink	2 strips 5/8" x 6"	random shapes for pulp
4" x 4"	Dk pink	2 strips 5/8" x 4"	random shapes for pulp
1½" x 4"	Black	1 strip 3/8" x 4"	triangles ¼"w x 3/8"h for seeds

WATERMELON FLOWERPOT

SHOPPING LIST

- ☐ Base item – 7½" dia x 5¼"h terra-cotta flowerpot
- ☐ Illustration board
- ☐ Acrylic paints – dark green, green, light green, pink, dark pink, and black

INSTRUCTIONS

Referring to table and photo, follow Basic Instructions (pgs. 2-9) to make a faux mosaic flowerpot.

Board	Color	First cut	Second cut
4" x 4"	Dk green sponged with green	2 strips ½" x 4"	10 squares ½" x ½" for rind
3" x 6"	Dk green sponged with green & lt green	3 strips ½" x 6"	31 squares ½" x ½" for rind
3" x 6"	Lt green	4 strips 3/8" x 6"	50 squares 3/8" x 3/8" for rind
10" x 10"	Pink	11 strips ½" x 10"	random shapes for pulp
10" x 10"	Dk pink	11 strips ½" x 10"	random shapes for pulp
3" x 4"	Black	3 strips 3/8" x 4"	triangles ¼"w x 3/8"h for seeds

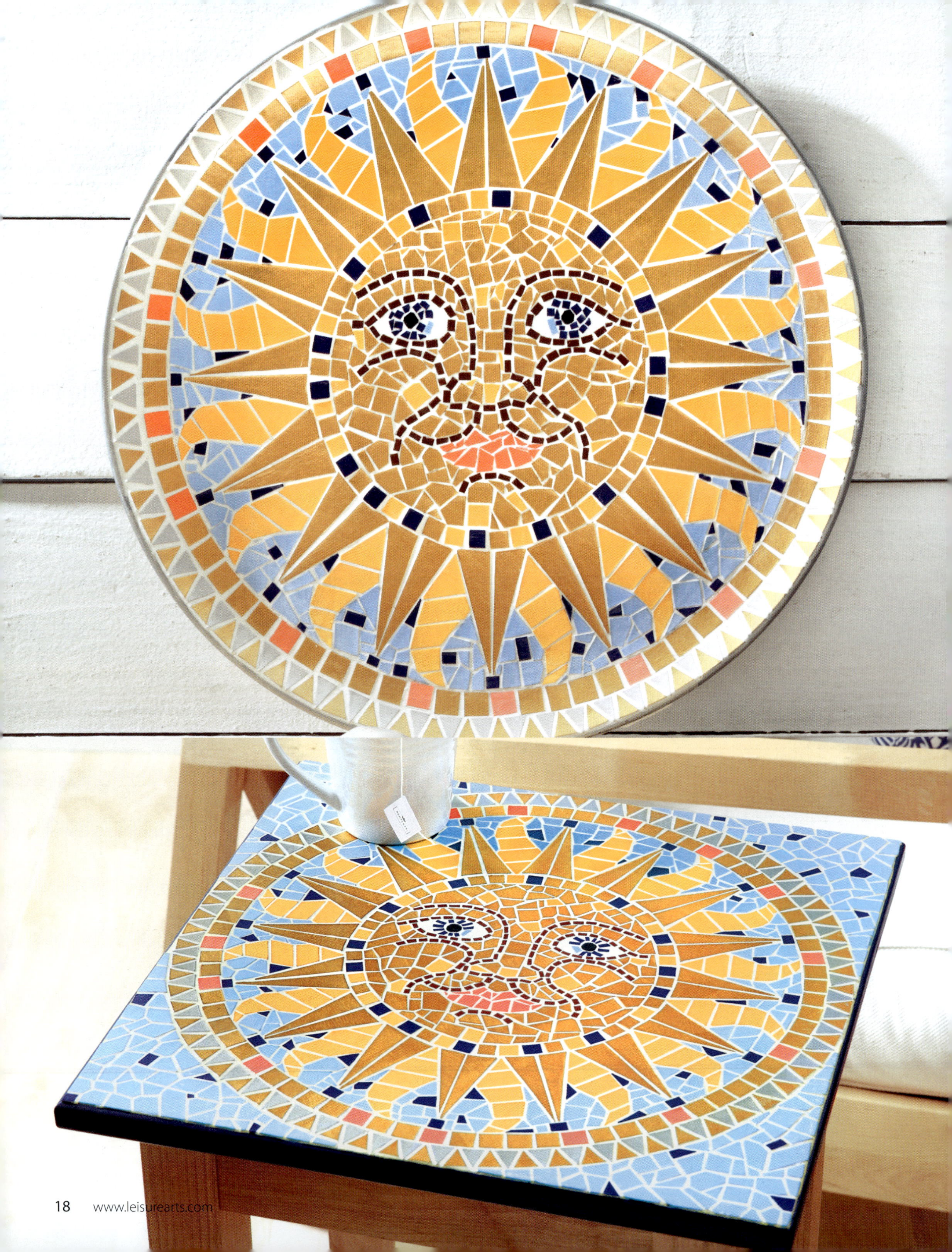

SUN FACE TRAY OR TABLE

SHOPPING LIST

- ☐ Base item – 16" dia metal pizza pan or 15¾" square table
- ☐ Illustration board
- ☐ Acrylic paints – metallic gold, metallic silver, black, white, dark brown, light blue, dark blue, coral, and yellow-orange
- ☐ Kraft paper for pizza pan (optional)

INSTRUCTIONS

Referring to table, photo, and Sun Face pattern (pgs. 30-31), follow Basic Instructions (pgs. 2-9) to make a faux mosaic tray or table top. If your pizza pan has holes in it, transfer the pattern to brown kraft paper. Glue kraft paper to the pizza pan before gluing on the illustration board pieces. We painted the edge of the table top dark blue.

Board	Color	First cut	Second cut
9" x 11"	Metallic gold	6 strips ½" x 9"	60 squares ½" x ½" and 68 triangles ½"w x ½"h for outer borders
		1 strip 5/8" x 9"	random shapes for face
		1 strip 3/8" x 9"	21 squares 3/8" x 3/8" for face border
		large triangles from pattern	
4" x 9"	Metallic silver	4 strips ½" x 9"	68 triangles ½"w x ½"h for outer border
1" x 4"	Black	1 strip 3/8" x 4"	2 random shapes for pupils
1" x 4"	White	1 strip ½" x 4"	random shapes for eyes
1" x 9"	Dk brown	2 strips ¼" x 9"	1/8" x ¼" rectangles for facial details
6" x 8"	Lt blue	7 strips for tray or 14 strips for table 3/8" x 8"	2 rectangles 1/8" x 3/8" for eye highlights and random shapes for background
8" x 8"	Dk blue	1 strip ¼" x 8"	random pieces for eyes
		1 strip 3/8" x 8"	15 squares 3/8" x 3/8" for face border
		7 strips for tray or 14 strips for table ½" x 8"	random shapes for background
1½" x 9"	Coral	2 strips ½" x 9"	16 squares ½" x ½" for outer border and random shapes for lips
3" x 9"	Yellow-Orange	1 strip 3/8" x 9"	14 squares 3/8" x 3/8" for face border and random shapes for face
		2 strips 5/8" x 9"	random shapes for rays

FESTIVE FLOWERPOT

SHOPPING LIST

- ☐ Base item – 4½" dia x 4"h terra-cotta flowerpot
- ☐ Illustration board
- ☐ Acrylic paints – yellow-orange, black, blue, green and dark green

INSTRUCTIONS

Referring to table and photo, follow Basic Instructions (pgs. 2-9) to make a faux mosaic flowerpot.

Board	Color	First cut	Second cut
3" x 8"	Yellow-orange	4 strips 3/8" x 8"	76 squares 3/8" x 3/8"
2" x 6"	Black	2 strips 3/8" x 6"	28 squares 3/8" x 3/8"
2" x 6"	Blue	2 strips 3/8" x 6"	27 squares 3/8" x 3/8"
3" x 4"	Green	2 strips 5/8" x 4"	19 triangles ½"w x 5/8"h
3" x 4"	Dk green	2 strips 5/8" x 4"	19 triangles ½"w x 5/8"h

FESTIVE CANDLE HOLDERS

SHOPPING LIST

- ☐ Base item – 3¼" dia 2½"h terra-cotta flowerpot
- ☐ Illustration board
- ☐ Acrylic paints – yellow-orange, black, blue, green, and dk green

INSTRUCTIONS

Referring to table and photo, follow Basic Instructions (pgs. 2-9) to make a faux mosaic candle holder.

Board	Color	First cut	Second cut
3" x 5"	Yellow-orange	1 strip 5/8" x 5"	13 triangles 5/8"w x 5/8"h
3" x 5"	Black	1 strip 5/8" x 5"	13 triangles ½"w x 5/8"h
3" x 6"	Blue	3 strips 3/8" x 6"	38 squares 3/8" x 3/8"
3" x 3"	Green	2 strips 3/8" x 3"	12 squares 3/8" x 3/8"
3" x 3"	Dk green	1 strip 3/8" x 3"	6 squares 3/8" x 3/8"

SUNFLOWER TRAY

SHOPPING LIST

- ☐ Base item – 14" dia wooden plate
- ☐ Illustration board
- ☐ Acrylic paints – yellow-orange, brown, tan, green, dk green, blue, and black

INSTRUCTIONS

Referring to table, photo, and Sunflower pattern (pg. 32), follow Basic Instructions (pgs. 2-9) to make a faux mosaic tray. Before spraying final coats of sealer, use a cotton swab to dot black paint on each brown and tan square in sunflower center.

Board	Color	First cut	Second cut
10" x 16"	Yellow-orange sponged with tan	16 strips ½" x 10"	random shapes for petals
		3 strips ¾" x 10"	37 triangles 1"w x ¾"h
5" x 6"	Brown	5 strips ½" x 6"	49 squares ½" x ½" for sunflower center
3" x 6"	Tan	3 strips ½" x 6"	34 squares ½" x ½" for sunflower center
5" x 5"	Green sponged with tan	4 strips 5/8" x 5"	31 squares 5/8" x 5/8" for border
4" x 5"	Dk green sponged with tan	3 strips 5/8" x 5"	23 squares 5/8" x 5/8" for border
4" x 8"	Blue sponged with tan	5 strips 3/8" x 8"	random shapes for background
3" x 9"	Black	2 strips 5/8" x 9"	37 triangles ¾"w x 5/8"h

SUNFLOWER FLOWERPOT

SHOPPING LIST

- ☐ Base item – 11" dia x 7½"h terra-cotta flowerpot
- ☐ Illustration board
- ☐ Acrylic paints – yellow-orange, brown, and tan

INSTRUCTIONS

Referring to table, photo, and Sunflower pattern (pg. 32), follow Basic Instructions (pgs. 2-9) to make a faux mosaic flowerpot. Make sure to wipe away all excess spackling between petals before the spackling dries – a craft knife, toothpick, or any slender, pointed object may make the job easier. Before spaying final coats of sealer, use a cotton swab to dot black paint on each brown and tan square in sunflower center.

Board	Color	First cut	Second cut
8" x 10"	Yellow-orange sponged with tan	10 strips ½" x 8"	random shapes for petals
3" x 5"	Brown	3 strips ½" x 5"	27 squares ½" x ½"
3" x 4"	Tan	3 strips ½" x 4"	18 squares ½" x ½"

DAISY FLOWERPOT

SHOPPING LIST

- ☐ Base item –9" dia x 7½"h terra-cotta flowerpot
- ☐ Illustration board
- ☐ Acrylic paints – white, black, yellow, green, dark green, blue, and dark blue

INSTRUCTIONS

Arranging and repeating leaves as desired, refer to photo, and Daisy pattern (pg. 31), and follow Basic Instructions (pgs. 2-9) to make a faux mosaic flowerpot.

Board	Color	First cut	Second cut
5" x 6"	White	5 strips ½" x 6"	random shapes for petals
10" x 12"	Black	6 strips ⅞" x 12"	62 squares ⅞" x ⅞" for rim
2" x 2"	Yellow	1 strip ⅜" x 2"	random shape for daisy center
3" x 3"	Green	leaf pieces from pattern	
3" x 3"	Dk green	leaf pieces from pattern	
10" x 15"	Blue	20 strips ⅝" x 10"	random shapes for background
10" x 15"	Dk blue	20 strips ⅝" x 10"	random shapes for background

PATTERNS

SUN FACE

DAISY

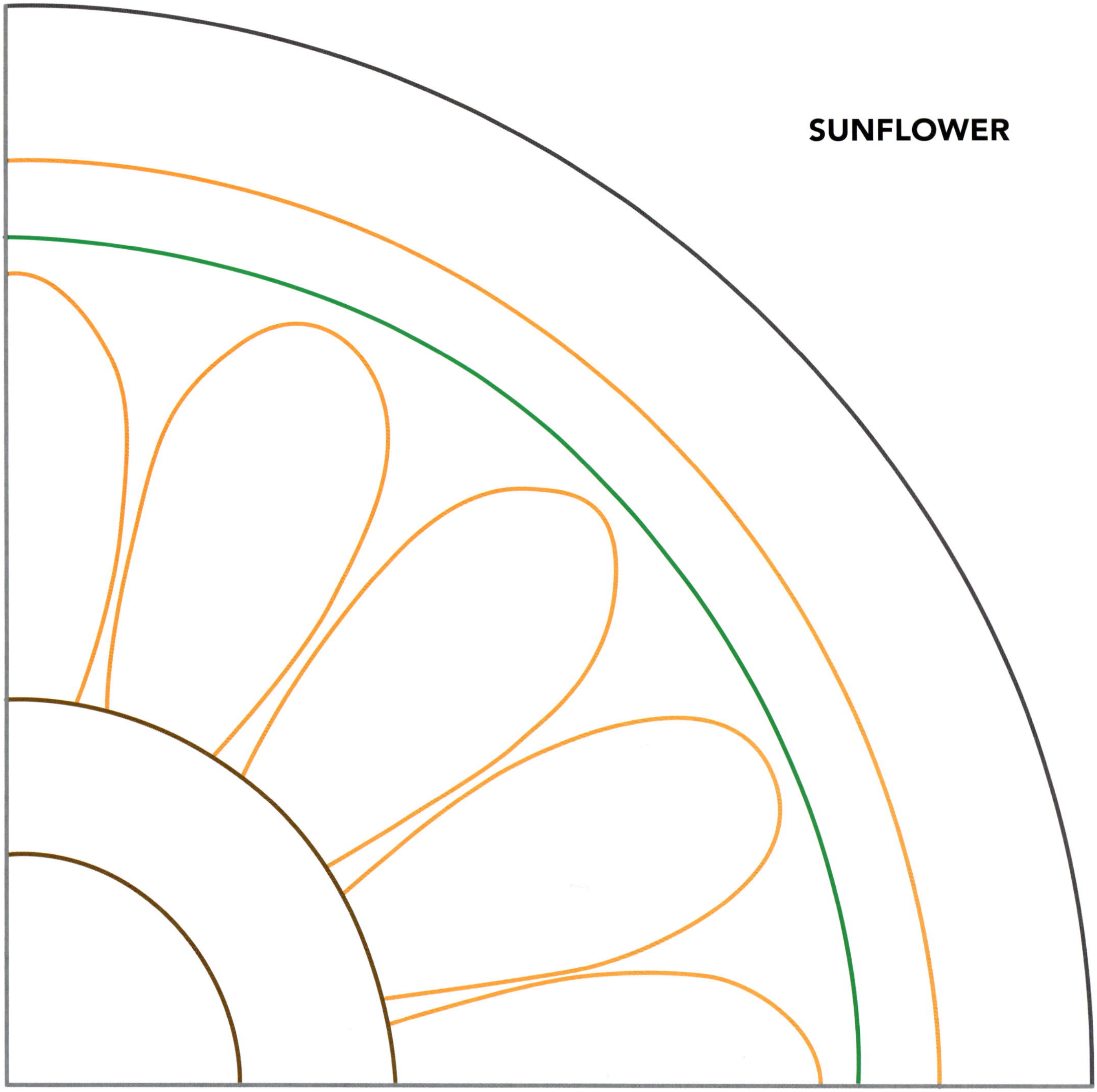

Production Team: Technical Writer – Lisa Lancaster; Editorial Writer – Susan Frantz Wiles; Senior Graphic Artist – Lora Puls; Graphic Artist – Kytanna McFarlin; Photostylist – Sondra Daniel; Photographer – Ken West.